DEPLORABLE ME!

DEPLORABLE ME!

An easy guide to deplorability

Bonita J. Bruce

XULON PRESS

Xulon Press
2301 Lucien Way #415
Maitland, FL 32751
407.339.4217
www.xulonpress.com

Paperback ISBN-13: 978-1-66281-979-7
Ebook ISBN-13: 978-1-66281-980-3

Dedication: To Patricia and Dale Shirley, whose unwavering friendship and love have continued to lift my wings, spirit, and joy. My life has been filled by their compassion and knowledge. I am forever grateful.

TABLE OF CONTENTS

INTRODUCTION

I am a Messianic Christian who is deeply in love with my Lord and Father. My life hasn't been easy, but it has always been interesting! Here is the abridged version:

1. I should not have survived my birth…but I did!

2. I should not have survived a brutal rape…but I did!

3. I should not have survived injuries sustained in a boating crash…but I did!

4. I should not have survived an attempted murder…but I did!

5. I should not have survived an attempted suicide…but I did!

I've written about all of this in an earlier book. The above happenings crept into my life, left their imprints upon my story, and shaped my life. More importantly, God's hands were all over me. Deplorable Me? Maybe! I am who I am because of who He is. Welcome to my life. I wish you were here!

Chapter I

FREEDOM OF SPEECH

The Constitution:

We the people of the United States, in order to form a more perfect Union, establish Justice, insure domestic tranquility, provide for the common defense, promote the general welfare and secure the blessings of liberty to ourselves and our posterity, do ordain and establish this Constitution of the United States of America.

The Bill of Rights:

Amendment I
Congress shall make no law respecting an establishment of religion, or prohibiting the free exercise thereof: or abridging the freedom of speech, or of the press: or the right of the people peaceably to assemble, and to petition the Government for a redress of grievance.

Amendment II
A well regulated Militia, being necessary to the
security of a free State, the right of the people to
keep and bear Arms, shall not be infringed.

Proverbs 13:3 – He who guards his mouth preserves
his life, but he who opens wide his lips shall have
destruction.

I believe in the fundamental right of free speech, but I cannot honor using this right to disparage and diminish the self-esteem or character of another. In the past four years, the use of free speech to ridicule another has become a hideously offensive form of this right.

Imagine how I felt when I recently became the recipient of this hurtful speech. I'd never met or conversed in any way with the speaker; she and I were complete strangers. However, this woman told me that I needed to add a new accomplishment to my resume. Up until recently, I had been known as a wife, a mother of three successful sons, a grandmother, a retired RN, a legal nurse consultant, an author, and a Christian counselor. I have worked since I was twelve, and I even put myself through high school and college.

Now, it seemed that I could add *"Deplorable"* to my resume! A few months later, a TV talk show personality decided to add *"Mentally Deranged"* to my lists of accomplishments. So, somehow, after fifty years of hard work and service, my attributes had been hijacked. I never saw that coming! And by whom?

All of a sudden, I would look in a mirror or watch a news broadcast and find myself defined by the words of a "former diplomat." The was the same person who could care less when she uttered the words, "What does it matter?" when young men, who were sworn to protect her and this country, gave their lives so she and her family could continue with theirs. This woman had lost her bid, for the second time, for the position of chief administrator of this country. She called me *deplorable!*

Deplorable – adj. 1. That can or would be deplored; regrettable 2. Very bad, wretched.

The second statement came from a TV talk show host—someone who makes her living sitting behind a table, talking about other people and stating her beliefs about them. This recent comment was aimed at the current vice president. She stated that those who believe in the power of prayer are "deranged." For someone who has been blessed many times by answered prayers, that's a very hard pill to swallow. As hard as it was for me, I know it hurt the heart of the vice president and all those who know the truth. Worse yet, that was the purpose of her statement. No filter! No accountability! No respect!

Deranged – v. 1. To upset the arrangement. 2. To make insane.

When I first heard these words targeted against me, my friends, and an elected representative of this country, I handled it poorly. It hurt my heart, and if it hurt my heart, just imagine what it did to God's! Those words sat so heavily on my heart, and maybe that was the intent of the women who spoke them. These women are well known for their bitterness and, in some cases, out and out hate speech. Their point of view is considered the only view!

As a Christian woman, I was their target. The "wretched" synopsis was especially hurtful and dealt with a subject matter that I hold very dear. I sincerely doubt that their words would have been aimed toward those of other religions. Without a doubt, Christians are their target.

Let me explain my "wretchedness," along with my "deranged" personality disorder.

I worked as a house cleaner, cleaning toilets in rental units, and as a teacher's aide until I was able to raise enough money to put myself through college to become an RN. Did I mention that I was a single mom at the time? I worked as an RN for thirty years. I now serve as a volunteer for battered women and children, trafficked young children, and the homeless. I consider my lifestyle a blessing to be able to do so! It's a God-given privilege that I don't take lightly.

I am not the woman who called another deranged or deplorable. I wouldn't consider that womanly. I am not the woman who held a mock severed, bloody head of the president of the United States in her hands. I am not the woman who yelled into a crowd, "Yes, I have thought of blowing up the White House." Nor am I the woman who yelled "IMPEACH, get in their face, and follow them into restaurants!" How unwomanly!

Have any of these women ever met me? Have they ever sat down and calmly talked with me? Have they ever made an effort to speak to those whose faith they have criticized? How can they possibly critique what they have not experienced?

1.   *Luke 18:32 (NKJV) – For He will be delivered to the Gentiles and will be mocked and insulted, and spit upon.*

2.   *Isaiah 51:7 (NKJV) – "Listen to Me, you who know righteousness, you people in whose heart is My law. Do not fear the reproach of men nor be afraid of their insults."*

I won't attempt to address the reasoning behind such statements. The reasoning is known only to those who spoke them. I can forgive, but I will always think of their words as an act of bullying, meant to hurt and frighten. For some, these women succeeded, and for others, we will certainly pray for you! Personally, I've taken my frustrations and placed them at the feet of Christ. That's what I do when the answers for which I am searching are beyond my capabilities.

Let's take a hard look at what makes our country so great.

The Constitution of the United States

> *We the people of the United States in order to form a more perfect Union, establish Justice, insure domestic tranquility, provide for the common defense, promote the general Welfare, and secure the blessings of Liberty to ourselves and our Posterity,*

*do ordain and establish this Constitution for the
United States of America.*

I've written the Constitution twice because it bears repeating. Reread it until you understand how precious it is, and then teach it to your children.

A final thought:

I believe God sets a path to be followed for each life. I also believe He gave us free will. Perhaps all concerned here should look deeply at the path they have chosen.

Chapter II

NO JOY

Absent - adj. 1. Not present; missing
2. Not existent; lacking

"I don't know if there is anything to look forward
to. I'm pretty hopeless, I guess."
– Kaylene Pasinsky (with permission)

Vice President Pence's statement on prayer was the catalyst for the "deranged" remarks. Well, I say, "Bless you, Mike Pence! Bless you, sir, for owning the fact that you speak to God daily." Now that's a "Me Too" movement I can relate with!

Yes, once more, I'll admit that I'm one of those "deranged" people who open their day with prayer. Each day begins with a praise for my Lord and Savior, followed by a prayer of thanksgiving for being awakened to a new day! During this time, I usually lift up all those who don't know God and ask Him to give them mercy and understanding. I lift up my children, my grandchildren, and my spouse, praying that they will be protected through the day.

My country, the president, the leaders of this country, and the nation of Israel are always in my final thoughts.

I have a "prayer closet," or as some call it, a War Room. Yes, I keep track of prayers prayed, prayers answered, and prayers "pending." Whether my prayers are answered or not, I always give thanks to my Father for hearing them, for I am well aware that they will be answered in His time.

Early each morning, my husband rises and prays the Amidah or Standing Prayer, which was composed around 450 BC. This prayer is repeated three times a day at the hours of prayer, 9:00 a.m., noon, and at 3:00 p.m. No, we are not Jewish; we just love the prayer. It's beautiful! The "Shema" is also a must for us every morning. If you are not familiar with it, read Deuteronomy 6:4-9.

I would like to tell the vice president, "In this society, which attempts to eradicate and blacken out any and all reference to the Almighty, you, sir, are an amazing, bright light and truly a man of courage." Blessed are those who neither attempt to hide nor deny the existence of God. Blessed are those who are not ashamed or fearful to speak of their faith.

I feel so sorry for those who, for whatever reason, don't come to the Lord in prayer. Sadly, they will never experience the power of prayer. It is such a privilege to know that I can come directly into the presence of God whenever, wherever, and under any circumstance. I don't need a "middle-man" or anyone to intercede for me. I don't need to be in any certain building or kneeling on a pew or on a prayer rug. I don't need to be dressed in a certain fashion. I am very blessed to have a direct relationship with my God. He is my Father. Why wouldn't I want to talk with Dad?

Those who dehumanize people of faith live without the joy and knowledge of answered prayer. Their lack of joy is evident by their brutal speech. They don't elevate people. They are more likely to yell, demand, shame, and coerce others. They always seem bitter and consumed in anger. They have only one agenda: their own. They have no reason to listen to the thoughts of another. Another's thoughts and relationship with God are totally dismantled. How could they hear the voice of God? They only hear their own voice. Every other sound is washed out. If these individuals don't get the response they want, they just keep the same ideas going for an endless amount of time.

You know when you hear the voice of God? When you are silent! I've been the recipient of many answered prayers, and yes, I've heard *Him* call my name. You know when I heard His voice? Not only when I was quiet, but when I was most in need.

I would much rather seek Him than try to power through this life by my own strength. The fact is, I did just that for years, and believe me, it did not go well!

If you hide in darkness, you will remain in darkness. If your words and actions align with God's, then you are truly blessed. It's a great idea to honestly search your heart; clear the clutter, bitterness, and anger from your life; and come boldly to the Father. He's waiting to hear from you. A little housekeeping of the heart can go a long way and can absolutely clear the air.

Let's look at another episode of stupidity. During the 2018 Emmy Awards, one of the presenters made this comment: "The only people who thank Jesus are Republicans and ex-crackheads." Well, thank God they do! Those who come through the depths of hell or the horrors of a life-destroying addiction have had the blessed moment of clarity and good sense to give praise and honor to the Almighty, and they came to His throne in a true spirit of thankfulness.

I pray you will understand that the things we have done do not define us. They don't have to be a statement of self. Life is about choices and their consequences. Author Robert Lewis Stevenson wrote, "Sooner or later everyone sits down to a banquet of consequences." Whenever that moment arises, I pray you won't be pre-occupied by how wonderful you are! Don't put God in a box…you can neither control nor contain Him. God is not a piece of metal you can wear around your neck. God is your refuge. You need Him because you can't fix yourself!

I not only learn from my mistakes and shortcomings—of which there are many—but I also learn from the mistakes of others. More importantly, I know where I can always go for help. What unbelievers don't understand—or perhaps won't try to understand—is that God already knows them. He knows their yesterdays, their today, and their tomorrows. Man's failure to understand the truth does not make the truth untrue.

To better understand this concept, let's take a look at the life of the beloved St. Paul.

1. Paul was a Pharisee and a Roman soldier, a scholar, and a Jew (Acts 22:3).

2. He became an Apostle to the Gentiles (Gal. 1:1).

3. He had been known as Saul (Acts 8:1-3, 13:9).

4. Paul supported the stoning of Stephen and the persecution of the early church (Acts 8:1-3).

5. Paul was converted on the road to Damascus (Acts 9:3-6).

Have you had a "Damascus" moment, where you encountered God and He changed your life? If not, maybe now is the time to pray for one. I suspect if we could see the difference our prayers could make in advance, we would be paralyzed by their impact!

I've been with God, and I've been without Him. I would deeply rather be with Him! I hate no one, nor do I wish them ill will. However, I do have a few questions for those who speak hate.

1. Have you ever known pure joy?

2. Have you ever offered joy to another? What did that look and feel like to you?

3. Do your words incite fear, anger, or hate?

4. Do you ask yourself if your words are hurtful or if they inflict feelings of guilt?

5.   Do your words demean another person or race?

6.   Do your words bully another?

CHAPTER III

WHO ARE THE LESSOR?

4. *Matthew 25:40 – And the King will answer and say to them, "Assuredly I say to you, insomuch as you did it to one of least of these My brethren, you did it to Me."*

Become more like the One whose image we bear.

Every child should be able to celebrate their birthday.

I'm going to devote this chapter to the one person who, more than anyone else, impacted my life with a sense of purpose, right and wrong, good and bad, distrust and total unconditional love…my niece and forever love, Donna Jean.

Donna was born with Cerebral Palsy. She could not walk and certainly needed assistance in every aspect of her life, except for the most important: pure, honest love. She made my heart sing! She taught me to love others without boundaries. She taught me to laugh even when my heart was breaking. Together, we could laugh as if no one else could hear us or understand why.

We were loud and proud! She was even the one who propelled me toward my career choice of nursing.

From the time Donna was born until she was three, I would babysit her. She could not speak in a language that anyone else could understand, but I like to think she spoke a language God understood. Even with her handicap, she sure could make her needs known.

During my babysitting, I'd spread a blanket on the floor, and that's where I'd be with her and her brothers. She could squirm off that blanket ever so fast, and when I'd catch up with her, she'd let out a squeal and off she'd go again.

Donna really disliked going to bed, so we'd cheat a little…well, maybe a lot. I'd get her brothers tucked in, and then it was time to "rock and roll"! Donna and I would turn up the radio and dance and sing—literally rock and roll. We loved Chuck Berry…well, one of us did. Most of the time, we would settle for country music, but not unless we were both tired. Soon, we'd had enough, and Donna and I would sit in the rocking chair. Slowly, she would fall asleep in my arms. So many times, I would just hold her and study her angelic face. This was how I came to understand the true meaning of love. Donna was truly a child of the Almighty. She convicted no one, and she loved and trusted those near her. She'd challenge your patience and then flash you a killer smile.

Life would soon take me far away, as life has a tendency to do. This beautiful child influenced my life more than anyone else has ever come close to doing, more than I could ever expect anyone doing again.

We lost Donna, as she has recently gone home to be with the LORD. The angels must have welcomed her with opened arms. I am positive that Donna now leaps with joy! When she tires, she can now crawl into the arms of God and rest in peaceful slumber.

Shalom, my darling. I will always thank God for allowing our lives to intertwine.

5   *Isaiah 35:6 – Then the lame shall leap like deer, and the tongue of the dumb shall sing.*

6   *Matthew 19:13-14 – Then the little children were brought to Him that He might put His hands on them and pray, but the disciples rebuked them. But Jesus said, "Let the little children come to Me, and do not forbid them, for of such is the kingdom of Heaven."*

Donna's disabilities strengthened my abilities. Because of her needs, I learned to use my God-given abilities and to share them with others who are in need of a helping hand. Through her eyes, I learned to look a little deeper. She convinced me to give of myself. I know that God's plan guided me, while Donna's heart encouraged me.

Rest now, my darling Donna. There is no illness in heaven. You are in the Great Physician's house now. Shalom.

Who is "less than" you? Who is not as great as you? Who is not as significant as you? When did you become so awe-inspiring? These are hard questions to ask another human being, and they are certainly very difficult to answer. Therefore, we have to examine our motives very deeply.

Unfortunately, we live in a superficial world where most of us judge others by their appearance, not the countenance of their heart. Some judge when they have no idea who the other person might truly be, or what values and intellect they possess. We marginalize. Some people even place those whom they cannot or will not accept on the very fringe of humanity or worse. Some give the "least" of humanity no human value.

I have a great deal of trouble understanding those who say only "certain" lives matter. Why do so many pick and choose which lives are more important than others? When was man given that right? Even if man had the right, what qualifications must one possess to qualify to be worthy of life? How can one decide who lives or who is to be cast away like garbage?

> 7. *Deuteronomy 27:25 – Cursed is the one who takes a bribe to slay an innocent person. And the people shall say Amen.*

Webster defines a bribe as anything, especially money, given or promised to induce a person to do something illegal or wrong. OK, that being said, why aren't aides, technicians, nurses, doctors, and even receptionists in abortion clinics held accountable for the wages they receive? I have painfully realized that these practices are legal in this country. After all, it's the law of the land! However, this is not the law of the Almighty God! Roe vs. Wade changed the law in this country, but it will never change the values and law of God. It will never be equal to the Word of God!

I've always wondered how so many can say they support life when they choose to deny it to those most vulnerable. For those who have no voice, I will be theirs. I won't allow myself to be silent as this nation throws away God's smallest and most helpless.

The forced death of 1.2 million per year cannot go unpunished. History will and has proved that the nations that sacrifice their young will not survive.

Who are to blame? All of us!

If you have sat silently since 1973…you are to blame.

If you voted into office those who supported this mandate… you are to blame.

If you supported the killing and dismemberment of the unborn… you are to blame.

If you were the recipient of tissue or a body part harvested from an unborn child…you are to blame.

If you allowed or taught students that "the product of human conception" was less than human and just a blob of tissue…you are to blame.

If you have claimed to be a Christian and sat in a church pew, or stood in a pulpit or behind a podium, and did not condemn infanticide…you are to blame.

There is more than enough blame and guilt to affect us all.

8. *Exodus 20:13 – You shall not kill.*

9. *Exodus 20:13ccer (The Schottenstein Edition Interlinear Chumash) – You shall no kill.*

> "Someone who truly believes in God as the Creator and Sustainer of human life will not commit murder. It is not coincidental that the modern world's accelerate loss of faith has been accompanied by an increasing cheapness of human life." – The Schottenstein Edition Interlinear Chumash

Take a long, hard look at Margaret Sanger. She wanted a new race. Here is a quote from her: "The mass of ignorant Negros still breed carelessly." Sanger was a racist whose goal was to decrease the population of African Americans. This was the beginning of Planned Parenthood. Don't be fooled. The same idea of reducing the populations exists today. Abortion is alive and just as insane today as it was when it was first spoken. The "perfect" race is being perfected, and we as a nation are too weak and too blind to see it.

For all those who chant "Black lives matter"—and they certainly do—you have a responsibility to call down Planned

Parenthood. Make no mistake, these people wanted you and your unborn scrubbed from this earth. This organization was founded on those mandates. Examine its motives and the motives of those who preach this filth. You are worth so much more than this hatred.

Here is another quote by Sanger: "The most merciful thing a family does to one of its infant members is to kill it." Sanger's entire theme was race and eugenics. "A better race through birth control." Millions bought into this idea without a second thought.

Those who have studied these statements know the effects they have had on families, education, communities, and an entire race. Hate-filled words always lead to hateful acts.

Margaret Sanger saw millions of unborn children as "less than."

The Chumash goes on to say that many have noted that the prohibition against murder seems to be so obvious that it hardly needs to be included in the Commandments. Unfortunately, in this country and from every pulpit, we have come to realize just how needed it is. The Commandment not to kill is not a suggestion; it is a command by the Almighty.

Murder was prohibited to all mankind, even to the most primitive societies. The question I ask is, when did it become anyone's *right* to murder? Who proclaimed it? My question to anyone who works in an abortion clinic would be, how do you see yourself after helping someone to murder a child?

Let's take a look at some of the reasons for having an abortion:

A child is not convenient at this time.

> Convenient - adj. Suited or favorable to a person's needs, comfort, or purpose.

> Question: Are the innocent child's needs, comfort, or purpose less important than yours?

This child is the product of rape / incest.

> Question: Is the infant in any way responsible for his/her conception?

> Question: Does the manner of an infant's conception make him/her less than human?

The "fetus" is less than perfect.

> Question: Who among us is perfect?

> Question: How does mere man define "perfect"?

> Thought: Man is created in God's image. Is God not perfect?

I'm too young, and I don't know who the father is!

> Over two thousand years ago, a fourteen-year-old Jewish girl faced the same problem. Yet she took

responsibility and trusted the Almighty God.
She was blessed beyond belief!

You may think I'm trivializing real issues, but I assure you, I am not. I've volunteered to serve the homeless, abused women and children, drug-addicted men and women, and unmarried pregnant teenagers as well as married women who choose abortions. I never tell them what to do; I just give them all the information and options. The choice is theirs to make.

I've seen it all first hand, and I've loved them all. I've witnessed their pain and their joy. My point is, before anyone chooses an abortion, we must allow them to be well equipped. Please give each individual the ability to make an informed decision. Let them be aware of all their options.

Some of the clinics and shelters offer the following to ensure their health and dignity: free vision and dental care; clothing; housing; food; education, along with assistance in writing a resume and how to dress for job interviews; diapers, baby clothing for two years, baby furniture, and car seats; and free ultrasounds that allow the mother to see her unborn child. These things are given freely and without prejudice as to race, ability, circumstance, or faith.

Please keep in mind that one selfish word or act can lead a person to overstepping all bounds of decent conduct. Once an abortion is complete, that little life is lost forever, and the memory of what is lost will also last forever. Also, think again about the victim of rape. Abortion after a rape re-victimizes the victim, literally re-wounding the wounded.

In many countries, the vulnerable are helpless against the whims and tantrums of their leaders and the thoughtless remarks of its population. I've heard over and over again how some in our society feel about the disabled—the lessor! These countries use abortion as a form of birth control. If the unborn child is "less than" they see as "normal," they just delete that innocent person.

Ignorance is not knowing something, while stupidity is knowing something but refusing to accept it.

Some diagnoses are clear; however, in such a case, it is essential to affirm that a disabled child is just as human as you or I and deserving of love, respect, and care. Our spiritual mandate is to care for the "least of these," God's children. I detest the word "disabled" when used to refer to another. People are equipped in many different ways, and we have very little insight into the minds of others. We must try cherishing each other before it's too late and we destroy one more human brother or sister. We are all in the human family, and no one has the "right" to end the life of another.

We are all made in the image of God, no matter how veiled that image may be behind physical deformities or mental limitations. Therefore, how can one possibly know the mental limitations of another? Text books were written by mere men, so we must ask ourselves, what is deformed or limited? How does man know the ways in which God creates? After all, His ways are unfathomable! The definition of "perfect" and "normal" are His.

Recently, a Hollywood actress proclaimed that women should deny sex until more lenient rulings for abortion are passed.

Wow! This brilliant woman just realized that abstinence led to no pregnancy. Imagine that!

Here's an article from *World News Service* that I found so uplifting for moms:

MRI's of the brains of mothers have shown that when they hear their baby's cry, areas of their brains are activated that are NOT activated in the brains of women who are not mothers. When mothers hear their baby crying, they are motivated more than anyone else to pick up the little one and talk to them, kiss them, rock them, or feed them. Studies conducted with 684 mothers from 11 countries showed this phenomenon is true across cultures. I find it strange that someone needed to conduct a study and MRI's to find out what every mom already knew!

What is "ordinary"? What is "good enough"? Every day, we are constantly bombarded with commercials crying out to try to convince us to buy the one thing that will make us more popular, more beautiful, or more acceptable. Politicians and actors are giving us "life instruction." For the love of all that is holy, be the person God intended you to be.

> 10. *Psalm 139:14 – For You formed my inward parts; You covered me in my mother's womb. I will praise You, for I am fearfully and wonderfully made; Marvelous are Your works, and that my soul knows very well.*

God wants us to have ordinary lives lived well! Only then will our lives will be extraordinary. Jesus said the kingdom of God is like a man who gave a banquet and made room for everyone who is willing to come—not just the movers and shakers, but also the poor, the crippled, the blind, and the lame, along with the weak and seemingly insignificant. Of course, there are no insignificant individuals. If you see anyone as insignificant, perhaps you need to search your soul…and you may be frightened by what you find there.

If you aren't aware of gracious living, let me point you toward the scene of the Last Supper. Christ—the only perfect person—washed the feet of His apostles. Here was God made flesh, washing the filth off the feet of sandal-clad fishermen. A complete act of humility and acceptance. An act of pure love shown to ordinary men by an *extraordinary God!*

Yeshua—Jesus—was born into poverty to a very young mother. He worked as an ordinary "blue collar" man. Yet He became the most *extraordinary* man ever to step foot on this earth.

How do you feel about unconditional acceptance? Our pets are absolute wonders, and I, for one, am so glad God thought of them! What or who else accepts you for you, the way your pets accept you? Bad hair or no hair, great smile or only a frown, clean and shiny or right off the garbage truck—they simply love you!

The greatness that is Him loves you unconditionally. Therefore, you are not limited by any society. There are times when you may feel broken, but you are not finished. If you only focus on your yesterdays or your past pain, you'll end up with an endless pile of "no good."

So, look up and fear not. Your tomorrow is from God.

Two last thoughts:

1. That which is loved is always beautiful.

2. When Christ walked the earth, He spent a large amount of His time with those whom society deemed "undesirable."

CHAPTER IV

WHO IS THIS GOD?

11. *John 10:4 – And when He brings out His own sheep,
    He goes before them, and the sheep follow Him, for
    they know His voice.*

You cannot stumble in the dark if you make God your light!

12. *Without having seen Him, you love Him. Without
    seeing Him now, but trusting in Him, you continue
    to be full of joy that is glorious beyond words, and
    you are receiving what you trust is your life mission,
    namely, your deliverance.*

Our hunger for meaning and love is only a journey to find God.

Let's begin at the beginning with a brief look at Genesis.

The simple idea that God created heaven and earth is one of the
most challenging of concepts. We live in a tremendously vast
galaxy spinning at 490,000 miles an hour, but it still requires
over 200 million years to make one rotation. Finite minds

cannot comprehend the infinite, and God is that infinite being. Add the fact that there are over a billion other galaxies, just like ours, in the universe, and you'll marvel at the remarkable order and efficiency that is required for all of it to exist.

Every ancient religion and almost every scientific and self-proclaimed atheist have opinions on the origin of this universe. I chose God.

You see, the simple fact that the Spirit of God was hovering over the surface of the waters before creation gives me the knowledge that God created the earth out of His great love, giving His people a unique place in it. He breathed life into man, and He wanted a place to fellowship with His people.

Because of my weaknesses, God has shown me great mercy and has actually strengthened my spirit. Once I surrendered to His will and not my own, I have learned so much about myself and my capabilities. When God lifted the "fog" from my life, I was able to see very clearly just who I am in Christ. My walk has been long, but looking back, I know how much that lifting was needed. Oh, I'm a continual work in progress, and just like every mortal, I will never know perfection in this lifetime. After all, good people don't go to heaven; forgiven sinners do.

Knowing my weakness, God saw the need to lift me up. We are instruments of the Lord, and He will use us, even as imperfect as we are.

Remember the story of the loaves and the fishes? Jesus took what was brought to Him and multiplied it. His provision was more than sufficient. Since we are laborers in His vineyard, we cannot take credit for His successes, and we also must not berate ourselves for our failures.

All of the individuals we meet throughout Scripture were ordinary people, but their relationship with an extraordinary God made them stand out.

Who does God use? Any broken person will do! He has even used a donkey to do His bidding.

In my life, I was fortunate to be able to be part of a prison ministry. What an amazing three years. I met so many "found" and recovering women. The crimes committed ranged from murder and grand theft to drug dealing and prostitution. Many of these women would never see freedom beyond barbed wire and prison walls, yet some spoke of unspeakable joy! If you have never heard the beauty of a choir of redeemed, Spirit-filled women, you have missed a blessed event. These were the voices of women who would not let fear stand in their way. They knew they were called back to their first love. This was the graciousness of re-birth. These women met God on *His* terms, accepted *His* will, and now were on a passionate pursuit of the Father.

God's love knows no boundaries, and His love never fails. This is God's promise, and He always keeps His promises.

In his letters to the Messianic community in Corinth, Paul gives us a definition of love, as written in the Complete Jewish Bible. He simply says, "I may speak in the tongues of men, even angels; but if I lack love, I have become merely brass or a cymbal clanging."

If you are of the understanding that God is judgmental and only condemns, or subjects everyone to a life of guilt, you must be careful. I realize that some churches are knee-deep in guilt, and if this is the case with you, please find a pastor who speaks of a loving, merciful God. If you do, you will know a greater joy.

The Bible is filled with the loving mercy of our Savior. He is the one who goes before you, and He will be with you always and will never leave you. God freely gives these promises to every believer. Man's greatest asset is God's everlasting love for His children.

Some people may seem to have their acts together, yet many of them are suffering, wrestling with major issues. They may be imprisoned by trauma from the past or anxiety concerning the future. Therefore, take the time to listen to others. You may be the one God has chosen to be their angel.

There are many opportunities to follow the Lord's call and to share His faithfulness and love. Let others see Christ in you. Through your spirit, let them find a safe landing away from their pain and suffering. Whenever you can, help someone make choices that align their lives with the way God has designed them…in His image! He created them in His own likeness, although they may not always recognize their Designer.

Share a new vision, yet don't let it come across as judgmental, preachy, self-righteous, or a personal agenda. This type of talk only brings more harm and is hurtful and negative. Don't add to their pain. As Paul says, don't be a cymbal clanging! You certainly don't want to rob a person of the opportunity of hearing a word from God. A few words may just change their day or even their lives. Ultimately, you must always rely on the Holy Spirit to do the heavy lifting.

In essence, God loves all of His daughters and sons, and He is always ready to forgive and erase our sins and shortcomings. All we need to do is to humble ourselves and ask Him!

Because we are made in His image, we have a responsibility to represent Him on this earth. This responsibility is a great deal to live up to, and as mortals, we often fall short. The beautiful truth is, God often gives us another chance to get it right! Along with this responsibility comes ownership, so build on the behavior you know is correct.

Therefore, it is always a privilege to share God's words with others and to affirm another person's worth. Preach the gospel at all times; when necessary use words.

We are always in God's view, and He is there in our brokenness. In this very sin-marred world, brokenness is a given. When we hurt, we are at a greater risk of beccoming deeply wounded, resentful, and even hate-filled. We must only remember that wherever we are, there He is! Although some issues are beyond our strength and ability to resolve, a miracle is waiting…just bring your mess to Christ. You alone cannot go toe to toe with Satan, so let Christ go to work for you.

The Son of God, Jesus Christ, was spit on, had thorns pressed into His scalp, and was beaten until His flesh fell to the ground. Man nailed His hands and feet, then raised His cross, which prevented His ability to even take a breath. Jesus did this all for us. It was the command of His Father, the Almighty, and He obeyed His Father. Jesus did this for the salvation of our souls, and by His death, He concurred ours. Before He died, His last thought was of us. We are now His redeemed. Eternal life is His gift to us, freely given, and today, abundant life is ours to choose.

> *Jeremiah 29:11-12 – For I know the thoughts that I think toward you, says the LORD, thoughts of peace and not of evil, to give you a future and a hope. Then you will call upon Me and go and pray to Me, and I will listen to you.*

I hope you have learned that you can call on and come before the Lord. Always be ready to receive His instructions. This is my prayer for you.

CHAPTER V

WASTED MOMENTS AND WICKED WORDS

Sooner or later, God will take over! Why wait
for later?

Have you ever thought about all the hours you've spent waiting?
Think of it. We wait for that "perfect" person to fulfill our lonely
lives. We wait for buses. Endless hours are spent waiting in gro-
cery stores, in bank lobbies, in medical offices…and then we
wait for test results! Put yourself in the mindset of the elderly
in nursing homes, waiting for months—sometimes even years—
for their child's visit.

Have you ever given freely of your time and energy to help
another fill the empty gaps in their lives, even when you have
nothing to gain from doing so? Or maybe you've spent empty
moment just trying to find where you "fit in."

Okay, so we are all flawed! Sometimes we go through our lives
just aimlessly wandering toward the next hour of our day. So,

let's take a deeper look at our lives, including our wasted hours and lost opportunities.

By wasted, I don't mean that these hours were spent doing absolutely nothing. Often, we can be very busy working without reaping anything. Who has sat at an office desk just to aimlessly stare at a computer screen? Who has sat in front of a TV without being able to recall one word of the program you just spent a half hour watching? Have you ever attended a college class listening to the professor, and when the class ended, you had no idea what he or she had said? And of course, you know what it is like to try listening to the pastor in the pulpit, while not even seeing him because your eyes were closed and your head bobbed toward your chest!

Since we are all human, we've all been in the above situations.

What happens next are the side effects of the aforementioned behavior—we absorb! We take it in and mindlessly absorb. We've drunk it in and didn't understand, ask, ponder, or question. We don't reflect on it because we can't reflect. After all, those in the know spoke so whatever it is cannot be questioned. We are told, *"It must be fact, and it must be true!"* In our society, we often follow the thoughts of those who don't know the truth, not knowing the impact their words and thoughts may have. Instead, we just agree with them. The politicians who make outrage remarks hope you will never question their words. And pastors and priests would never allow false teachings to flow from a pulpit! Teachers and professors could never have personal agendas and claim them as genuine. How could any of the very well-educated professionals speak for personal gain?

Oh, but they do. What a waste of time!

One of the blackest marks on recent American history was the character assassination of the Honorable Brett Kavanaugh. I have interviewed, worked with, and taken depositions from rape victims. I have performed rape kit examinations, and I myself was a victim of a brutal rape at age sixteen. In all my past experiences, never have I heard such garbage!

I watched the proceedings of his hearing, and not for one moment did I believe Ms. Christine Blasey Ford. However, I wanted to believe her. I want all victims of hate crimes to be believed. It takes great courage to come forward, and I want the stories of these individuals told. Yet Ms. Ford made a mockery of the victim's right to be heard and the perpetrators to be punished. During the hearing, she was unable to confirm any of the charges she brought forward. Hours of wasted dialog.

I can still recall every detail of my own attack, and every detail vividly. Those to whom I attended as an ER nurse or a counselor could do the same. In fact, if conscience during their attacks, 99 percent of late teens and adults have excellent recall.

This country and all those who falsely accused Judge Kavanaugh of the unthinkable should beg his forgiveness. An apology is also due to his wife and daughters.

Benjamin Franklin said it best: "Never ruin an apology with an excuse." An apology only works if it is communicated to the other person in such a way that that person can clearly understand and receive it. An apology should:

a. express regret (i.e. "I'm sorry.")

b. express wrongdoing (i.e. "I was wrong.")

c. make restitution (i.e. "What can you do to make it right?")

d. request forgiveness (i.e. "Will you please forgive me?")

Here's a tip on forgiveness: make forgiveness a request; never demand it. The choice to forgive is that of the other person. Never waste an apology!

In Kavanaugh's case, those proceedings will make it much more difficult for those who will be brutalized in the future to come forward. We took a giant step backwards due to the frivolous acts of a few. I, for one, am ashamed of the hate speech spewed out in those chambers.

I pray that next time, those who reign over our hallowed halls will remember that their words and actions can always align their hearts with God. Of course, you must first align yourself with God through your own actions and words. I don't know the heart of any man, but I do hear what they say. I also know that hatred corrodes the container in which it is carried.

Recently, we've experienced many school shootings, drive-by shootings, and gang murders where the victims have been dismembered and tossed away like garbage. My heart broke for the rabbi whose synagogue was attacked during Shabbat services on October 27, 2018. Eleven members of the Tree of Life

Synagogue in Pittsburg lost their lives. The rabbi spoke of the "Evil in my Holy Place." Evil did indeed walk in that day!

Take a breath and think. The past half century, in this country, has absolutely seen more acts of violence, hatred, bigotry, antisemitism, and out and out hatred toward our own citizens than ever before in our history. Or, could the evil in the past just have been politely hidden and hushed from the public arena? Actually, it was never hushed. Hatred of another's color, heritage, or faith have been a part of everyone's past. Yes, everyone has suffered in one way or another by the unkind word, act, or abuse of others.

True friends are now found in metal boxes ruled by thumbs. So many now voice their hatred immediately, while those who hear it mindlessly accept it as meaningful speech. They follow the ugly wherever it leads them, parroting the same phrases over and over. Unfortunately, the media is a great medium for hate speech. TV anchors, talk show hosts, and Hollywood actors repeat whatever they think will increase their ratings with no thought how their words may impact others. Very few are original thinkers, as most just echo the ugly! It all falls under the heading of "Extreme Opinion"! There are no facts, just hateful opinions spun as truth in hopes that others will not search for the hidden reality.

It is very difficult to believe that those who speak hate really want to be remembered for some of the words they've uttered. We live in an era where every syllable uttered is recorded for all posterity. Someday you will be somebody's grandparent! How are you going to feel when a child remembers Grandma for yelling, "IMPEACH, IMPEACH, IMPEACH"? Perhaps some little boy or girl will only know that prayer is "Bull S___." And remember, they will!

The lists go on and on. I think it's a great idea to consider your words carefully. Take the time to ponder the nemesis behind your speech. C. S. Lewis wrote fictional accounts of Satan and his minions conspiring to plant hideous thoughts in our minds. I, for one, believe in Satan, and I also believe he uses anyone who is willing to spread his dark spiritual warfare as his instrument. Keep a sober mind and be watchful; listen carefully before someone attempts to devour your thoughts.

16 *Galatians 6:10 – As we have opportunity, let us do good to all people.*

I certainly cannot change the mindset of the people who have uttered such distorted views and values, but I will never buy into the misguided attitudes of a few. Instead, I choose to pray for my enemies. I suppose this is certainly not what these people would do for me, but it's my choice to treat them a certain way. I can't change their minds—that is way above my "pay grade." However, I will listen to their points of view and pray they will do the same for me.

Recently, some of our non-working representatives in Washington labeled the Christian Bible as "hate speech." My heart hit the floor on that one. So, now the Word of God is hate speech? One thing is for sure: those who agreed with this statement will never see a vote from me again. I will always honor my Judeo-Christian roots.

Christ prayed for those who persecuted Him…and I will do the same once I work through the pain the above statement caused me. Meanwhile, to those who called me "deplorable," perhaps you might want to rethink your comment. Your brutal choice of words just may be used in your eulogy.

God already has their names written in His book, and in the end, they will be read aloud! No amount of time will erase them. Only when the Holy Spirit takes up residence in their hearts will those words be remembered no more.

Chapter VI

PRAYER

Connection with the Great Communicator

Growing up in the Catholic religion, the only way I was taught to pray was to memorize prayers written by some other person whom I had never met. That scared me because sometimes these prayers were about things I didn't understand, and some were even aimed at a person I knew nothing about. Even worse, a great deal of the time, I had to memorize prayers in a foreign language.

It took me many years before I actually realized that prayer is talking directly to God. No memorized prayers, no prayer mat, no special clothing, no statues, no specific buildings or rooms, and no third party was necessary to carry my prayer to my God. Prayer is just He and I, one to one, whether all alone or in a crowd. I learned that I could talk to Him whenever and wherever I chose. How beautiful and freeing is that?

Dr. Moody Stuart, a great man of prayer, once drew up a set of rules to guide him in his prayers. Among these rules is this: "Pray till you pray!" When I first read this, I knew exactly what he meant.

In prayer, you should remove all the inhibitions, negative thoughts, and interruptions and just speak from the heart. Pray, and don't leave anything unsaid. Tell God who you are. He already knows, but He wants to know that you know. Also, never start your prayers with "if" or "when." Remember who you're talking to. May His will be done. Don't challenge God. Rather, trust Him, even if He doesn't answer immediately. He knows your needs. Could it be that perhaps what you want is not in your best interest? Never bargain with your Father. You know the old "I'll do this if you do that"? That isn't going to turn out well! Depend on God. After all is said and done, be aware that your future prayer could have an enormous impact on your life.

Have you ever heard the phrase "armpit Christians"? These are the people you see in churches who only attend to be seen and usually have a Bible tucked under their arm. However, if asked, they could not recall what is written on its pages! True Christians love the Lord, love His words, and are known by God as His sheep. The same idea is true of prayer. When you pray, don't be hypocritical. You do not need to preach on street corners, clothed is sackcloth and covered in ashes. God already knows your name and how you present yourself.

When you pray in earnest, find a quiet place where you can search your thoughts and be specific. Don't be a show off! There is no need to shout or yell your prayer, for He hears your whispers. Perhaps if you're quiet, you may be deeply blessed to hear His whisper in return.

Have you ever read the story of Nabeel Qureshi? If you haven't, it's well worth your time. Nabeel is a former believer in Islam who converted to Christianity. He dedicated one of his books to his sister, who was not yet a believer of Christianity. He stated, "I am begging God for the day that we can worship Him together." I am very familiar with that prayer. I pray it daily for my sons and their families. I thank God for their conversions. Oh, it hasn't happened yet, but I *know* it will. You see, I'm a praying mother; therefore, their conversions will come to pass. I surely don't when or how, but for me, there is no "if."

I don't resent the phrase "Thy will be done"; rather, I embrace it. I always pray for the ill, for the lost, for those who have no hope, and for those who think prayer has no power. I certainly can't convert them, but once again, that's way above my job description. God does the conversion; I am just His messenger.

I also know there are a great many who do not believe in the laying on of hands. That's very sad. However, I understand their viewpoint because I was once one who did not accept this concept…key word, was! I do so now when I'm led by the Holy Spirit. I can already hear the groans from the unbelievers. I am truly sorry for your unbelief, but I personally know the power of the Holy Spirit and will not discount it. One can also "lay hands" on oneself. Prayer can absolutely line up every cell with God's will.

Also, speaking in a prayer language is an enormous gift. God understands this language, and that is all that needs to be said!

It is so very sad that so many people go through life not knowing how to pray. There are those who don't understand or anticipate hearing or seeing the effects of prayer. Unfortunately, unbelievers often become cynical and cannot or will not accept anyone who does believe in the power of prayer. I pray for them in hopes that God will expand their thinking.

Christianity isn't synonymous with being silent. We should stand up and be counted. Recently, I read an article that mentioned a type W or "walk on water" personality. Could this be the God gene? This personality type does not imply that one has the same makeup as God; it simply means that if God called you to do so, and you claimed to trust Him, would you get out of that boat? Something to ponder.

Prayer is a perfect union with God, and there is no special preparation or dress code for it. Come just as you are.

Pray, and then pray some more!

Jesus said, "You, therefore, pray like this."

> *Our Father in heaven*
> *May your name be kept holy*
> *May your Kingdom come,*
> *Your will be done on earth as in heaven.*
> *Give us the food we need today*
> *Forgive us what we have done wrong,*

As we too have forgiven those who have wronged us.
And do not lead us into hard testing,
But keep us safe from the Evil One.
For kingship, power and glory are yours
forever. AMEN

– Matthew 6:7-13 (CJB, Complete Jewish Bible)

The KJV says it a little differently, and either version is just fine with Him!

CHAPTER VII

ME AND MY DEPLORABLE FRIENDS

God promises that if we seek Him with all our hearts, we will find Him, and that those who are His sheep will hear His voice.

Perhaps those who call others "deplorable," "crazy," and "deranged" are just too busy hearing themselves talk that they've blotted out the voice of God!

– B. J. Bruce

In his book, *The Call*, Os Guinness describes a moment when Sir Winston Churchill sat with some friends near a fireplace on a cold evening. He gazed at the pine logs crackling, hissing, and spitting as they burned. He simply said, "I know why logs spit. I know what it is to be consumed."

I believe we've all experienced some "all-consuming moment" in life. It's all part of the journey. Some of those moments are filled with unspeakable joy, while others are nearly devastating, to say the least.

The problem addressed here is how some people never work through those moments that seem to be devastating, holding onto those moments until they indeed become overwhelming. They cannot let go and release the pain of what they feel to be unbearable.

The "could have been" or "should be" take over their every thought. The "only ifs" soon turn to the "why me?" If all these thoughts are left unchecked, then blame takes over. Sadly, the blame is usually placed on others and not how one perceives his or her ideas and anger. Hatred sets in, and a lifetime of contempt can now become "all-consuming." A malicious cycle has been formed.

This is how I remember another influential person in my life. What did I learn from her behavior? What not to do! Those characteristics that she adhered to sickened me. I did not become the person she thought I should. I've held myself to a different level.

Why do I bring this up? Well, I have a question for the former first lady and secretary of state. How do you want your grandchildren to remember you? How do you want to be eulogized? What will be their most cherished memory of you? If you continue to belittle those you don't even know and refer to them as so far beneath you, then that will be how you will be remembered by those who once loved and held you so dear. Don't let bigotry and prejudices define you.

I'm going to jump into Hillary's world of deplorability. I want to introduce to you some of my friends who share the "basket" with me. Together, we form a boatload of deplorability. All of us share some common goals. We honor God, our families, and this country. We all come from different backgrounds, and we celebrate the differences. We all have had different experiences, interests, and careers. Some are married, some are divorced, and some are single. Those who have no clue say we all shop at Walmart and have a smelly, strange odor. Some very uninformed souls believe we are all Caucasian, married women who only follow the whims of our GOP spouses! Those statements have to make one wonder just how Republican women of color survive in Hillary's world? Hillary called us puppets. Somehow, she doesn't understand just how independent most of us truly are.

As for me, I am a former Democrat turned Republican, white, married woman who is college-educated and a mom of three sons. I managed to hold down a very demanding career and maintained a home, all while being married to a naval officer for twenty years, which ended in divorce. I am now remarried and retired after thirty years as an RN. I did it all without the help of any nannies, maids, or secretaries. My now husband, as well as my sons, all have different viewpoints and goals. Rarely do we vote the same party lines. In fact, most of the time, my husband and I cancel out each other's votes. However, we still manage to love and support each other, even when we don't agree. We have a healthy respect for our individuality.

Remember the childhood chant "Sticks and stones may break my bones, but words will never hurt me"? Sometimes misguided words did hurt, and they may have had the same effect as a welt from a stick or stone. Yet that was then and this is now. As an adult, I have decided to put away childish name calling and refuse to allow the words of the childish behavior of a few to weigh me down. I know who I am in the eyes of those who love and respect me, but more importantly, I know who I am in the eyes of God.

There is a great need for this country to experience a renovation of the heart. We could relinquish the unnecessary and focus on what is necessary. I truly wish that some of those mentioned above would take some time to calmly speak with true Christian leaders. What they learn may soften their speech and their hearts. These gifted leaders come in all races, and they are from all nations. Perhaps they may even start and end their days the same way a great many of us deplorables do—on our knees. Many of us end each day giving thanks, even when painful and hurtful speech has been thrown our way.

Other deplorables include not only the clergy, but doctors, nurses, and first responders. These are the ones you call first when danger and illness come your way. You certainly wouldn't call a congressman when your life is in danger.

Some of my favorite deplorable people are teachers, whether the ones in schools or the ones at kitchen tables. One teacher I know has tutored many a young child with special needs in her home for years, and even after she retired, she continued to do so. One friend of mine homeschooled all of her eight children. Yes, I said eight! She had no nanny or housekeeper, and she lost her husband when her youngest was two. This sainted woman also volunteered at our local food bank twice a week. Every day, she thanked God for her blessings.

Let me tell you about another sister who takes my breath away. She is the mother of two sons, both born with muscular dystrophy. She is their only caregiver, as her husband left them when the going got rough! Still, she goes about her very physically challenging, hectic life without complaint. She also never misses her Sunday service, even though she has to manage two wheelchairs. With all that, I have never seen her without a smile and a hug if someone else needs one. She also gives out free hugs!

With all this in mind. I pray that the former first lady, along with the "woke" generation, will think twice before they speak such hateful and demeaning words again. We deplorables are a very decisive group, and we would love to help you with your language skills.

Here are just a few noteworthy deplorables:

The Rev. David Jeremiah; Pastors John, Diane, and Matthew Hagee; Pastor Mark Biltz; Pastor Rabbi Jonathan Cahn; Rabbi Jason Sobel; Pastor Robert Jeffries; The entire family of the blessed late Billy Graham; Mr. R. Larry Moyer; Al and Verna Barton; Mrs. Ann Voyles; Mrs. Mary Pulid; Mrs. Elizabeth Tenbrink; Mr. Mike Rurup; and Patricia and Dale Shirley; just to name a few.

Others who are always willing to help:

All the volunteers from Union Gospel, the Salvation Army, Samaritan's Purse, and missionaries from around the world.

Let us never forget the wounded warriors and our veterans who have given their all for this great nation. We must support them and their families. You see, we deplorables love God and country. We love those who are without hope, joy, or freedom, and especially those without peace in their hearts.

For my wonderful deplorable friends, here is my thought for you:

Frances de Sale very wisely wrote, "Do not look ahead to what may happen tomorrow, The same everlasting Father who cares for you today will take care of your tomorrows and every day. Either He will shield you from suffering or He will give you unwavering strength that you may bear it. Be at peace, then, and set aside all anxious thoughts and worries."

I agree! Shalom Aleichem (peace to you), especially to those who do not know Him.

CHAPTER VIII

QUESTIONS AND ANSWERS

Question – seeking to learn or in testing another's knowledge; a matter open to discussion or inquiry; a point being debated.

Remember, all choices have consequences.

1. What single step would you take today to minimize the regret factor at the end of your life?

2. Who knows everything about you?

3. Would another person truly love you even if they knew the true you?

4. Do you grieve the person you wish you were?

5. Is what you do all you can do?

6. What is the one thing you would be willing to give of yourself to help another?

7. Do you have anger issues? If you do, write them down and hold them up to Christ. You will see a new point of view!

8. Have you ever known great, unconditional love or joy?

9. Have you ever given great, unconditional love or joy?

10. Have your feelings toward the disabled, the oppressed, or the challenged been less understanding than you know they should be?

11. What type of people do you hold as "less valuable"?

12. Would you consider volunteering some time and energy to help the less fortunate (and not just for a photo or selfish reason)?

13. Do you feel this country is suffering an avalanche of "godlessness"?

14. Is what we knew as good now thought of as bad?

15. Is lawlessness and hatred the new definition of righteousness and love?

16. Why did Jesus die? Read 2 Corinthians 5:18-19.

17. Can anything separate us from God's love for us? Read Romans 8:38-39.

18. What does the name Yeshua mean? Salvation!

Here are just a few words to ponder. Take the time to think very hard about what they may mean to you.

Abort, anarchy, Antifa, artificial intelligence, assimilate, KKK, nefarious, terrorist, socialism, vilification, woke.

You may want to look up the origin of Planned Parenthood and Margaret Sanger. Afterward, ask yourself why so many Democratic-run cities in this country are now hotbeds of violence? Why is this country in such turmoil? Then ask yourself one more question: In one of his statements, former Vice President Biden said, "All men are created by, oh you know, that thing." What are your thoughts and feelings concerning that one statement? Think long and hard, then ask yourself again, why is this country in turmoil?

CHAPTER IX

AND IN CONCLUSION

Conclusion: noun - A final decision, a deduction. An end.

Challenges don't make you who you are; they reveal who you are. Think about it. How many times have you heard or said, "He makes me so mad." No, you were already mad. He just revealed it!

I guarantee, if you are blessed to be able to read the Torah and begin to live it, your life will be forever changed. I know, because I have and I do. Since I wasn't Jewish, someone asked me why I still read it. "To learn," was my answer. Once I read it, I knew exactly why I was drawn to it. When a giant dose of earthly reality hits you, a strong faith can sustain you.

Mark 4:17 says it so much better than I… "And they have no root in themselves, and so endure only for a time. Afterwards, when tribulation or persecution arises for the word's sake, immediately they stumble."

Mark 4:37-41 continues,

> And a great windstorm arose, and the waves beat into the boat, so that it was already filling. But He was in the stern, asleep on a pillow. And they awoke Him and said to Him, "Teacher, do you not care that we are perishing?" Then He arose and rebuked the wind, and said to the sea, "Peace, be still!" And the wind ceased and there was a great calm. And He said to them, "Why are you so fearful? How is it that you have no faith?" And they feared exceedingly, and said to one another, "Who can this be, that even the wind and the sea obey Him?"

My job is not to determine how the gospel will be received, but to declare it and to share it with you. God alone will see to the proper results. So, when Satan comes to fuel the fires of hate, lawlessness, greed, and despair, seek God's Word. Keep His words in your heart and be forever blessed.

Here are a few ideas that will bless you. If you sanction abortions, don't dare to misguide others. Don't tell people how much you pray and how you cherish His words. El Shaddai (God Almighty) *never* gave you permission to destroy the unborn. *Never!*

If you truly don't know President Trump, you may want to read about the Hebrides Revival. Then think about what Isaiah 44:3 has to say. "For I will pour water on the thirsty land (a land in great need of saving) and streams on the dry ground. I will pour My Spirit on your offspring's and on descendants."

Why don't we take a moment and pray for our president, the justices, and our senators and representatives? Let us pray that they be diligent and never defame God's words. May we ask that they be honest and mindful of their every word, and that God will let them realize that they are mere men and not gods. I pray that they actually will start their days on their knees and not just say that they do. How they speak will always let you know how they truly feel and if it is right and just.

This country has weathered many storms, and 2020 is no exception. The challenges we have faced in 2020 have been like no other. We all found ourselves in unchartered territory, secluded and left to our own thoughts. So many young men and women have been manipulated by the words of several of those in leadership positions—words meant to control and destroy. God has been removed from this country. We now hear candidates for our highest offices deny Him. These people not only want to remove God from our nation, but they want complete control of every aspect of our lives. Wake up, America, and discern the times.

> 17. *2 Chronicles 7:13-14 – "If I shut up Heaven that there is no rain, or if I command the locust to devour the land, or if I send pestilence among My people, when My people, over whom, MY name is called, humble themselves and pray and seek My face and turn from their ways, then I will hear*

from Heaven and will forgive their sin and will heal their land."

In 2020, the horrifying death of Mr. George Floyd left many of us reeling in pain and disgust. His family suffered a nearly unbearable loss, and we saw so much hatred and destruction in the days that followed. Unfortunately, so many low-life politicians used this pain to stoke the fires of pure hatred for this country. Mr. Floyd's brother spoke through his tears and anguish, stating that the violence must stop. *And it must!* Terrence Floyd said it so beautifully: "Can we try another way? Let's switch it up, ya'll. Let's switch it up. Do this peacefully, please…Let's do this another way."

Here is my belief system:

If you accept a belief, you reap a thought.

If you sow a thought, you reap an attitude.

If you sow an attitude, you reap an action.

If you sow an action, you reap a habit.

If you sow a habit, you reap a character.

If you sow a character, you reap a destiny.

May your destiny be filled with love, understanding, joy, many blessings, and *peace.*